Get set... GO!

Bread

Judy Bastyra

Photography by Michael Michaels

Contents

Watts Books

London • New York • Sydney

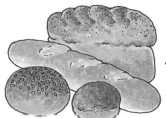

About bread

Bread dough is made of
flour, yeast and water.
Flour comes from grains,
such as wheat, barley and rye.

white flour

wholemeal flour

The yeast makes the bread rise.

yeast

Bread comes in all shapes in sizes.
Sometimes bread is made into loaves...

...sometimes it is made into rolls.

How to knead dough

✔ Sprinkle some flour on your work surface.

✔ Flatten the dough with the heel of your hand.

✔ Fold it in half and flatten it again.

✔ Repeat this for 10 minutes until the dough is smooth and shiny.

✔ Put the dough in a greased bowl, cover with a cloth and leave in a warm place to double in size, or rise, for about 1 hour.

10 golden cooking rules

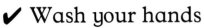

✔ Wash your hands  before you begin.

✔  Read the whole recipe carefully.

✔ Make sure you have all the ingredients and equipment you need.

✔ Measure out the ingredients carefully.

✔ Allow at least 15 minutes time for the oven to warm up.

✔ Wear an apron to protect your clothes.

✔ Use a separate spoon if you want to taste the mixture.

✔ Always use oven gloves
to put something in the oven and to take it out.

✔ Always turn the handle of

a saucepan on the stove to one side.

✔ Finally, don't forget to do the washing up!

GUIDE TO THE MEASUREMENTS USED
tbl/tbls – *tablespoon/s*   tsp/tsps – *teaspoon/s*
g – *grams*   ml – *millilitres*

Wherever you see this symbol,
it means that you should
ask for help from an adult.

One rise white bread

Get ready

✔ 1 tsp dry active yeast
✔ Half a tsp salt
✔ 350g plain flour
✔ 240ml warm water
✔ Greased baking tray
✔ Mixing bowl
✔ Wooden spoon
✔ Tea towel
✔ SET OVEN TO 230°C/450°F/GAS MARK 8

...Get set

Mix the dry ingredients in the bowl.
Add the water slowly and mix to form a dough.
Knead for 10 minutes (see page 3).
Cover the dough with the tea towel.
Leave it to rise in a warm place.

⇒✿⇒✿⇒✿ *Go!*

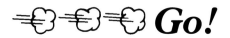

Form the dough into an oval shape.
Bake it on the baking tray for 30 minutes.
Take the bread out of the oven and leave to cool.

Banana bread

Get ready

✔ 75g soft margarine
✔ 175g brown sugar
✔ 1 egg
✔ 225g plain flour
✔ 2 tsps baking powder
✔ 4 ripe bananas, mashed
✔ Wooden spoon
✔ Mixing bowl
✔ Bread tin
✔ Greaseproof paper
✔ SET OVEN TO 180°C/350°F/GAS MARK 4

...Get set

Line the tin with the greaseproof paper.
Beat the sugar and margarine together.
Add the egg and mix until creamy.
Slowly mix in the flour.
Stir in the baking powder and bananas.

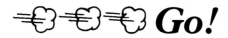 **Go!**

Spoon the mixture into the tin.
Bake in the centre of the oven for 1 hour.

Savoury breads

Get ready

✔ 450g one rise bread dough (see page 6)

✔ 1 egg, beaten

✔ Pastry brush

✔ SET THE OVEN TO 230°C/450°F/GAS MARK 8

✔ Savoury fillings, such as grated cheese, mixed herbs, chopped ham and olives

✔ Greased baking tray

...Get set

Divide the dough into four balls.
Flatten each ball with your hand.
Sprinkle different fillings into each one.
Knead the dough for 5 minutes.

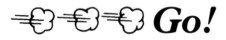 **Go!**

Make different shapes with the dough, such as letters, plaits and twists.
Brush the tops with egg.
Cook on the baking tray for 15–20 minutes.

Sweet bread animals

Get ready

- ✔ 450g one rise bread dough (see page 6)
- ✔ 3 tbls mixed glacé fruits, chopped
- ✔ 2 tbls dessiccated coconut
- ✔ Angelica, raisins, glacé cherries to decorate
- ✔ 1 egg, beaten
- ✔ Greased baking tray
- ✔ Pastry brush
- ✔ SET THE OVEN TO 230°C/450°F/GAS MARK 8

...Get set

Sprinkle flour on to your work surface.
Flatten the dough with your hand.
Shake over the mixed fruits and the coconut.
Knead the dough until well mixed.

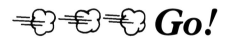 **Go!**

Shape the dough into animals such as a fish.
Add faces with raisins, angelica and glacé cherries
Brush with the egg and bake for 15–20 minutes.

Garlic bread caterpillar

Get ready

✔ 2 peeled garlic cloves
✔ 50g soft butter
✔ 1 small French loaf
✔ 1 cucumber, sliced
✔ 2 cherry tomatoes
✔ Garlic press
✔ Mixing bowl
✔ Bread knife
✔ Silver foil
✔ 2 wooden toothpicks
✔ SET THE OVEN TO 200°C/400°F/GAS MARK 6

...Get set

Crush the garlic with the press.
Mix it with the butter in the bowl.
Make deep cuts in the bread all the way along.
Spread the garlic butter inside.

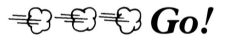 **Go!**

Wrap the loaf in foil and bake for 15 minutes.
Remove the foil and add cucumber in the cuts.
Attach tomato eyes with the toothpicks.

Chocolate pots

Get ready

- ✔ 4 slices white bread
- ✔ Chocolate spread
- ✔ 2 eggs
- ✔ 180ml milk
- ✔ Round biscuit cutter
- ✔ SET THE OVEN TO 180°C/350°F/GAS MARK 4

- ✔ Knife
- ✔ Measuring jug
- ✔ 4 ovenproof ramekins
- ✔ Baking sheet

...Get set

Cut eight bread circles with the biscuit cutter.
Spread each one with chocolate.
Put two bread circles in each ramekin.
Crack the eggs in the jug and beat.
Add the milk and pour over the bread.

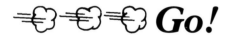 Go!

Put the ramekins on a baking sheet.
Bake in the oven for 20–25 minutes until set.

Rude face rolls

Get ready

✔ Bread rolls

✔ Butter or margarine

✔ Ham, sausage, salami, cheese for fillings

✔ Knife

✔ Radishes, cucumber, olives, tomatoes, carrots, cress for decoration

✔ Wooden toothpicks

...Get set

Cut each roll half way across to make a mouth.
Spread margarine or butter inside.
Cut the meat into tongue shapes.
Cut the cheese into teeth shapes.
Arrange them inside the rolls.

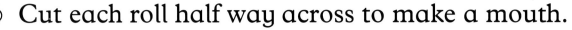

Go!

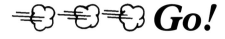

Add vegetable eyes, noses, ears, hair and hats using the wooden toothpicks where necessary. (Remember to take them out before eating them!)

Bread pictures

Get ready

✔ Brown or white sliced bread
✔ Knife
✔ Paper
✔ Pencil

✔ Toppings, such as cream and cottage cheese, lemon curd, chocolate spread
✔ Fruit, vegetables, salami, egg cress, sprinkles to decorate

...Get set

Plan your picture on the paper.
Spread a sweet or a savoury topping on each slice of bread.

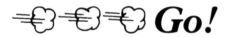 *Go!*

Use your plan to decorate the bread.
Put savoury decorations on a savoury topping.
Put sweet decorations on a sweet topping.

Eggy train

Get ready

✔ Brown or white sliced bread

✔ Soft butter

✔ 4 hard boiled eggs

✔ 2 tbls mayonnaise

✔ Marmite

✔ Salt and pepper

✔ Carrots, celery, pepper, tomatoes, twiglets to decorate

✔ Fork

✔ Knife

✔ Mixing bowl

...Get set

Mash the eggs with one teaspoon of butter.
Mix in the mayonnaise and season.
Butter the bread and sandwich together with layers of egg mixture and marmite.

Go!

Cut off the crusts.
Cut each sandwich
into carriage-shaped rectangles.
Decorate the tops and add carrot wheels.

Index

First published in 1995 by
Watts Books
96 Leonard Street
London EC2A 4RH

Franklin Watts Australia
14 Mars Road
Lane Cove
NSW 2066

Editor: Pippa Pollard
Design: Ruth Levy
Cover design: Shoba Mucha
Artwork: Ruth Levy

Special thanks to Charles
Bradley, assistant food designer
and stylist.
Thanks also to Aroma for
crockery used pp. 7, 17.

A CIP catalogue record for this
book is available from the
British Library

Dewey Decimal Classification:
641.8

UK ISBN 0 7496 1494 3

10 9 8 7 6 5 4 3 2 1

© 1995 Watts Books

Printed in Malaysia

24

Fife
C O U N C I L
King's Road Primary School
Rosyth - Tel: 313470